12/95

Pride and Promise:
The Harlem Renaissance

edited by Kathryn Cryan Hicks

© Discovery Enterprises, Ltd.
Lowell, Massachusetts
1993

All rights reserved. No part of this book may be reproduced, stored in a retrieval system, or transmitted in any form or by any means, electronic, mechanical, photocopied, recorded, or otherwise, without prior written permission of the authors or publisher, except for brief quotes and illustrations used for review purposes.

© Discovery Enterprises, Ltd., Lowell, MA 1993

ISBN 1-878668-30-7 paperback edition

Library of Congress Catalog Card Number 93-72240

10   9   8   7   6   5   4   3   2   1

Printed in the United States of America

Subject Reference Guide:

Harlem Renaissance – Juvenile Literature
African American History
African American Writers, Artists, Musicians

Photo Credits

World War I soldiers returning to the United States after fighting with French military. Courtesy: National Archives.

Acknowledgments

"Fifty Years" by James Weldon Johnson. © 1917 by James Weldon Johnson

"Negro Soldiers" by Roscoe Jamison, *Crisis*, Sept. 1917

"Oriflamme" by Jessie Fauset, *Crisis*, Jan. 1920
(Also appeared in *The Book of Negro Poetry*, 1931 and 1959)

"To Usward" by Gwendolyn Bennett, *Opportunity*, May 1924

"Saturday's Child" by Countee Cullen. Reprinted by permission of GRM Associates, Inc., Agents for the Estate of Ida M. Cullen. From *Color* by Countee Cullen. © 1925 by Harper & Brothers; copyright renewed 1953 by Ida M. Cullen.

"The Negro Speaks of Rivers", "The Weary Blues" from *Selected Poems* by Langston Hughes. © 1926 by Alfred A. Knopf, Inc. and renewed 1954 by Langston Hughes. Reprinted by permission of the publisher.

"Dream Deferred" ("Harlem") from *The Panther and the Lash* by Langston Hughes. © 1951 by Langston Hughes. Reprinted by permission of Alfred A. Knopf, Inc.

"Song of the Son" by Jean Toomer, *Cane.*
© 1951 by Liveright Publishers, NY. (There is a 1975 edition)

"The Lynching" by Claud McKay, *Selected Poems by Claud McKay.* © 1953 by Twayne Publishers

811.5208
PRI
1993

Table of Contents

Dedication

To Phil
my husband and best friend

Foreword

Most of us picture the decade of the twenties as a time of fun and excitement—fast dances, new rhythms and liberation from stuffy Victorian ways. No place typified this image of the "Roaring Twenties" with its nightlife, music and dance, more than Harlem, a predominantly African American neighborhood of New York City. Beneath that image of gaiety, however, simmered social unrest due to racial hostility, lack of housing and unemployment.

Yet in the midst of this social turmoil there flourished a new spirit of black pride nourished on promise and hope. That spirit, manifested as the Harlem Renaissance, ushered in a bounty of African American literature, art and music. Historians date the period of the Harlem Renaissance from World War I until the Depression, yet the conditions which brought it about had been developing for over fifty years.

Fifty Years
(1863-1913)
by James Weldon Johnson

*On the Fiftieth Anniversary of the Signing of the
Emancipation Proclamation*

O brothers mine, today we stand
  Where half a century sweeps our ken,
Since God, through Lincoln's ready hand,
  Struck off our bonds and made us men.
Just fifty years—a winter's day—
  As runs the history of a race;
Yet, as we look back o'er the way,
  How distant seems our starting place!

Look farther back! Three centuries!
  To where a naked, shivering score,
Snatched from their haunts across the seas,
  Stood, wild-eyed, on Virginia's shore.

For never let the thought arise
  That we are here on sufferance bare;
Outcasts, asylumed 'neath these skies,
  And aliens without part or share.

This land is ours by right of birth,
  This land is ours by right of toil;
We helped to turn its virgin earth,
  Our sweat is in its fruitful soil.

Where once the tangled forest stood—
  Where flourished once rank weed and thorn—
Behold the path-traced, peaceful wood,
  The cotton white, the yellow corn.

To gain these fruits that have been earned,
  To hold these fields that have been won,
Our arms have strained, our backs have burned,
  Bent bare beneath a ruthless sun.

That Banner which is now the type
　　Of victory on field and flood—
Remember, its first crimson stripe
　　Was dyed by Attucks'* willing blood.

And never yet has come the cry—
　　When that fair flag has been assailed—
For men to do, for men to die,
　　That we have faltered or have failed.

We've helped to bear it, rent and torn,
　　Through many a hot-breath'd battle breeze
Held in our hands, it has been borne
　　And planted far across the seas.

And never yet—O haughty Land,
　　Let us, at least, for this be praised—
Has one black, treason-guided hand
　　Ever against that flag been raised.

Then should we speak but servile words,
　　Or shall we hang our heads in shame?
Stand back of new-come foreign hordes,
　　And fear our heritage to claim?

No! stand erect and without fear,
　　And for our foes let this suffice—
We've bought a rightful sonship here,
　　And we have more than paid the price.

And yet, my brothers, well I know
　　The tethered feet, the pinioned wings,
The spirit bowed beneath the blow,
　　The heart grown faint from wounds and stings;

The staggering force of brutish might,
　　That strikes and leaves us stunned and dazed;
The long, vain waiting through the night
　　To hear some voice for justice raised.

Full well I know the hour when hope
　　Sinks dead, and round us everywhere

Hangs stifling darkness, and we grope
  With hands uplifted in despair.

Courage! Look out, beyond, and see
  The far horizon's beckoning span!
Faith in your God-known destiny!
  We are a part of some great plan.

Because the tongues of Garrison
  And Phillips now are cold in death,
Think you their work can be undone?
  Or quenched the fires lit by their breath?

Think you that John Brown's spirit stops?
  That Lovejoy was but idly slain?
Or do you think those precious drops
  From Lincoln's heart were shed in vain?

That for which millions prayed and sighed,
  That for which tens of thousands fought,
For which so many freely died,
  God cannot let it come to naught.

The Migration North

The Emancipation Proclamation of 1863 may have made slavery illegal, but African Americans in the South remained enslaved in economic ways for many years after President Lincoln signed this important manifesto. White landowners managed to keep black sharecroppers in perpetual debt. A lack of education and training, together with the existing racial prejudice, made it next to impossible for black citizens to find employment with decent wages.

In addition to the economic inequities, African Americans at that time faced an increase in racial violence. Lynchings were on the rise and the feared Ku Klux Klan (formed in 1866) grew more powerful. Floods and the boll weevil brought devastation to many crops in the South making food scarce.

It wasn't until 1914, with the outbreak of war in Europe that many southern blacks were able to improve their situations. The War put a temporary halt to European immigration to the United States, and industry focused its recruiting efforts on the disenfranchised southern workers. Demand for labor in the northern industrial cities provided a reasonable escape from the deplorable conditions in the South.

The Migration of Negroes
by W.E. Burghardt Du Bois
The Crisis, June 1917

"Much has been written of the recent migration of colored people from the South to the North, but there have been very few attempts to give a definite, coherent picture of the whole movement. Aided by the funds of the National Association for the Advancement of Colored People, *The Crisis* has attempted to put into concrete form such knowledge as we have of this movement.

"The data at hand are vague and have been collected from a hundred different sources. While the margin of error is large, the actual information which we have gathered is most valuable.

"First, as to the number who have migrated to the North, there is wide difference of opinion. Our own conclusion is that about 250,000 colored workmen have come northward. This figure has been builded up from reports like the following which we take from various personal sources and local newspaper accounts:

"From Alabama, 60,000 able-bodied wokers; from Savannah, Ga., 3,000; Montgomery, Ala., 2,000; West Point, Ala., 1,000; Americus, Ga., 3,000; Jefferson County, Ala., 10,000; West Point, Miss., 1,000; South Carolina, 27,000; West Point, Ga., 800; Macon, Ga., 3,000; Florida, 15,000; Notasulga, Ala., 3,000. From Abbeville, S.C., 'by the hundreds all through the fall and winter.' From Muskogee, Okla., '5,000 from the city and vicinity.' One day '1,022 Negroes from the South came into Cincinnati.' An estimate of the Boston,

Mass., *Transcript* gives 200,000 immigrants. From Southwest Georgia, 5,000. *Bradstreet's* estimate: 'An immense migration.' From Birmingham, Ala., 10,000; Arlington, Ga., 500; Waycross, Ga., 900; Bessemer, Ala., 3,000; Columbus, Ga., 500; Tuscaloosa, Ala., 2,500; Dawson, Ga., 1,500. Immigrants to Springfield, Mass., 500; to Chicago, Ill., 50,000, and 'coming in at the rate of 10,000 in two weeks,' (estimate of the Chicago *American*).

"As to the reasons of the migration, undoubtedly, the immediate cause was economic, and the movement began because of floods in middle Alabama and Mississippi and because the latest devastation of the boll weevil came in these same districts.

"A second economic cause was the cutting off of immigration from Europe to the North and the consequently wide-spread demand for common labor. The U.S. Department of Labor writes:

> A representative of this department has made an investigation in regard thereto, but a report has not been printed for general distribution. It may be stated, however, that most of the help imported from the South has been employed by railroad companies, packing houses, foundries, factories, automobile plants, in the northern States as far west as Nebraska. At the present time the U.S. Employment Service is not co-operating in the direction of Negro help to the north.

"The third reason has been outbreaks of mob violence in northern and southwestern Georgia and in western South Carolina.

"These have been the three immediate causes, but back of them is, undoubtedly, the general dissatisfaction with the conditions in the South. Individuals have given us the following reasons for migration from certain points:

"Montgomery, Ala., better wages, lack of employment, bad treatment; West Point, Ala., boll weevil; Americus and Cartersville, Ga., lynchings, schools, bad treatment, low wages; Birmingham, Ala., right to vote, discontent, bad treatment, low wages; Fairburn, Ga., low wages, bad treatment; Sanford, Fla., low wages, bad treatment; Anniston, Ala., low wages, bad treatment; Jefferson County, Ala., low wages, bad treatment; West Point, Miss., low wages; La Grange, Ga., low wages, bad treatment; Washington, Ga., low wages, schools; Newnan, Ga., low wages; Jackson, Ga., protection, schools; Covington, Ga., low wages; Montezuma, Ga., low wages, oppression; Tallahassee, Fla., unrest, conditions, low wages; Honeapath, S.C., low wages; Douglassville, Ga., bad treatment, poor schools; Raleigh, N.C., protection and the right to vote; West Point, Ga., boll weevil; Franklin, Ga., bad treatment and fear of lynching; Lithonia, Ga., low wages, bad treatment; Rome, Ga., injustice in the courts, low wages, lack of privileges, schools; Live Oak, Fla., low wages, bad treatment; Columbus, Ga., low wages, bad treatment; Atlanta, Ga., low wages; Jackson, Miss., low wages, bad treatment; Augusta, Ga., low wages, bad treatment; Nashville, Tenn., low wages; Meridian, Miss., low wages, discrimination; New Orleans, La., low wages; Mobile, Ala., low wages; South Atlanta, Ga., schools, freedom; Macon, Ga., low wages; Valdosta, Ga., unemployment, bad treatment; Cuthbert, Ga., bad treatment; Wadley, Ga., schools, civil rights; Gainesville, Ga., low wages, bad treatment.

"To this we may add certain general statements from colored leaders thoroughly conversant with conditions in their communities and in some cases with large parts of the South.

"A colored man of Sumter, S.C. says: 'The immediate occasion of the migration is, of course, the opportunity in the North, now at last open to us, for industrial betterment. The real causes are the conditions which we have had to bear because there was no escape.'

"These conditions he sums up as the destruction of the Negroes' political rights, the curtailment of his civil rights, the lack of protection of life, liberty and property, low wages, the Jim Crow car, residential and labor segregation laws, poor educational facilities.

"From Oklahoma we learn that Negroes are migrating because of threatened segregation laws and mob violence.

"A colored man from Georgia states: 'In my opinion the strongest factor in this migration is a desire to escape harsh and unfair treatment, to secure a larger degree of personal liberty, better advantages for children, and a living wage.'

"The A. M. E. Ministers' Alliance of Birmingham, Ala., names seven causes for the migration: 'Prejudice, disfranchisement, Jim Crow cars, lynching, bad treatment on the farms, the boll weevil, the floods of 1916.'

"A colored business man of North Carolina believes: 'There is a silent influence operating in the hearts of the growing class of intelligent Negroes that the insurmountable barriers of caste unnecessarily fetter the opportunities to which every living soul is entitled, namely, a fair chance to earn an honest living and educate his children and be protected by the laws.'

"In many sections of Mississippi the boll weevil destroyed the cotton crop; rains and high waters in the spring destroyed other crops.

"A well-known investigator reports: 'Nothing else seemed left for hundreds of the colored tenants to do but to go into the cities or to the North to earn even their food. Nothing was left on the farms and the landowners could not or would not make any further advances. From the country and even from the cities in these unfortunate sections colored people have in many cases streamed northward.'

"The centers of this migration have been at Jackson, Hattiesburg, and Meridian, Miss., and many have sacrificed property in order to get away.

"A widely-traveled and intelligent colored man writes:

> I recently made a trip through the South as far down as New Orleans, La., and I saw hundreds who were making their way northward. When in New Orleans, I learned that there were about

14

800 in the city from the inland district waiting to go, and who expected to leave during the next week. I went with a friend down where I could meet some of the leaders and talk with them. I met them, and they informed me that they were willing to go anywhere rather than continue to live like they had been. These were heading toward Chicago. I was shocked at the statement made by some of them as to how they lived on those big inland farms, and how badly they were treated by the whites. Many of these men were in overalls. I told them that they were unprepared for the climate; but they were willing to run any risk to get where they might breathe freer. Who blames them?

"Many of the southern whites, through their newspapers, are confirming this general unrest. A white woman says:

That which a regard for common justice, fair play, human rights could not accomplish, a fear for our bank account is doing, and we are asking: Why is the Negro dissatisfied? What can we do to keep him in the South? We can't afford to let him go; he means too much for us—financially. He works for little; his upkeep costs us little, for we can house him in any kind of shack, and make him pay us well for that; we do not have to be careful of his living conditions; he is good-natured, long-suffering, and if he should happen to give us trouble we can cope with that and the law will uphold us in anything we do.

"The Columbia, S.C. *State* asks: 'If you thought you might be lynched by mistake, would you remain in South Carolina? Ask yourself that question if you dare.'

"The Greenville, S.C., *Piedmont* feels that,

> The truth might as well be faced, and the truth is that the treatment of the Negro in the South must change or the South will lose the Negro.

"The Greenville, S.C., *News* says:

> The Abbeville outrage may yet prove more of an economic crime than an offense against the peace and dignity of the state. Where is our labor to come from if not from these people who have lived here beside us for so many generations? Immigration has been a distinct failure in the South; it is expressly declared to be against the policy of South Carolina by our laws.

"It is interesting to note that this migration is apparently a mass movement and not a movement of the leaders. The wave of economic distress and social unrest has pushed past the conservative advice of the Negro preacher, teacher and professional man, and the colored laborers and artisans have determined to find a way for themselves. For instance, a colored Mississippi preacher says:

> The leaders of the race are powerless to prevent his going. They had nothing to do with it, and, indeed, all of them, for obvious reasons, are op-

16

posed to the exodus. The movement started without any head from the masses, and such movements are always significant.

"The character of the people who are going varies, of course, but as the Birmingham, Ala., *Age-Herald* remarks:

It is not the riff-raff of the race, the worthless Negroes, who are leaving in such large numbers. There are, to be sure, many poor Negroes among them who have little more than the clothes on their backs, but others have property and good positions which they are sacrificing in order to get away at the first opportunity.

Various reasons are assigned for the migration of Negroes from the South to the North. It was believed for a while that they were lured away by the glowing reports of labor agents who promised high wages, easy work, and better living conditions. But there is something more behind their going, something that lies deeper than a temporary discontent and the wish to try a new environment merely for the sake of a free trip on the railroads. . . .

The entire Negro population of the South seems to be deeply affected. The fact that many Negroes who went North without sufficient funds and without clothing to keep them warm have suffered severely and have died in large numbers, has not checked the tide leaving the South. It was expected that the Negroes would come back, sorry that they ever left, but comparatively few have returned. With the approach of warmer weather the number going North will increase.

"How great this migration will eventually prove depends upon a number of things. The entrance of the United States into the war will undoubtedly have some effect. When the war ends it is doubtful if the labor shortage in Europe will allow a very large migration to the United States for a generation or more. This will mean increased demand for colored laborers in the North. A writer in the New York *Evening Globe* predicts that 1917 will see 400,000 of the better class of Negro workers come to the North.

"At any rate, we face here a social change among American Negroes of great moment, and one which needs to be watched with intelligent interest."

Years of Strife

The years 1916 to 1920 saw over half a million African Americans migrating to northern cities. Some of these migrants were hired by war-related industries; some filled openings left vacant by workers who joined the armed services. Some were hired by companies whose regular workers were on strike. Many African Americans were employed for the first time and felt an economic security they had never known. In addition, they were able to offer family members in the South a refuge.

The refuge, however, was not always a safe one. The North had its share of racial violence. On July 2, 1917, one of the nation's worst race riots occurred in East St. Louis, Illinois. Over 150 black citizens were killed, six thousand driven from their homes; many homes burned as the occupants struggled to leave them.

A few weeks after the riot in East St. Louis, over ten thousand blacks staged a silent march down Fifth Avenue to protest racial violence. With only the sound of muffled drums the children, all dressed in white, marched first, followed by the women all dressed in white. Then came the men dressed in black carrying banners of protest and a streamer which stretched the width of the street proclaiming "Your hands are full of blood." The parade moved in silence and was

ALBUQUERQUE ACADEMY
LIBRARY

watched in silence by thousands of white citizens, many of them with tears in their eyes.

The Negro Silent Parade
The Crisis, September 1917

"On the afternoon of Saturday July 28, a vast body of Negroes marched through the streets of New York in silent protest against the recent race riots and outrages. The *New York American* says:

"In silent protest against the recent killing of Negroes in race riots in Waco, Memphis and East St. Louis, 15,000 Negroes marched here yesterday afternoon. The parade formed in Fifth avenue and marched from Fifty-seventh street to Madison Square.

"Placards carried by boy scouts, aged men and by women and children explained the purpose of the demonstration.

"A detailed account of the causes for which the parade was held is given as follows by the *New York Times*:

"During the progress of the march circulars were distributed among the crowds telling of the purpose which brought the Negroes together. Under the caption, 'Why Do We March?' the circular read, in part, as follows:

'We march because by the grace of God and the force of truth the dangerous, hampering walls of prejudice and inhuman injustices must fall.

'We march because we want to make impossible a repetition of Waco, Memphis, and East St. Louis by arousing the conscience of the country, and to bring the murderers of our brothers, sisters and innocent children to justice.

'We march because we deem it a crime to be silent in the face of such barbaric acts.

'We march because we are thoroughly opposed to Jim Crow cars, etc., segregation, discrimination, disfranchisement, lynching, and the host of evils that are forced on us. It is time that the spirit of Christ should be manifested in the making and execution of laws.

'We march because we want our children to live in a better land and enjoy fairer conditions than have fallen to our lot.

'We march in memory of our butchered dead, the massacre of honest toilers who were removing the reproach of laziness and thriftlessness hurled at the entire race. They died to prove our worthiness to live. We live in spite of death shadowing us and ours. We prosper in the face of the most unwarranted and illegal oppression.

'We march because the growing consciousness and solidarity of race, coupled with sorrow and discrimination, have made us one; a union that may never be dissolved in spite of shallow-brained agitators, scheming pundits and political tricksters who secure a fleeting popularity and uncertain financial support by promoting the disunion of a people who ought to consider themselves as one.'

"Although the paraders marched by in silence their sentiments were proclaimed by many mottoes, a complete list of which follows:

'Memphis and Waco—Centers of American Culture?'·

21

'Alabama needs 75,000 Ballots to elect 10 Congressmen. Minnesota needs 300,000. How do they do it?'

'350,000 voters in the South have as much political power as the 1,500,000 voters of New York State. How do they do it?'

'Each white man in the South by disfranchising the black working man casts from 3 to 13 times as many ballots as YOU.'

'Georgia and New Jersey have the same vote for President. Georgia casts 80,000 votes; New Jersey casts 430,000.'

'Make America safe for Democracy.'

'Taxation without representation is tyranny.'

'Thou shalt not kill.'

'Thou shalt not bear false witness against thy neighbor.'

'We hold these truths to be self-evident that all men are created equal. That they are endowed by their Creator with certain unalienable rights. That among these are LIFE, LIBERTY and the pursuit of HAPPINESS.'

'If you are of African descent tear off this corner.'

'America has lynched without trial 2,867 Negroes in 31 years and not a single murderer has suffered.'

'200,000 black men fought for your liberty in the Civil War.'

'The first blood for American Independence was shed by a Negro—Crispus Attucks.'

'We have fought for the liberty of white Americans in 6 wars; our reward is East St. Louis.'

'12,000 of us fought with Jackson at New Orleans.' "

The "Harlem Hellfighters"

When the U.S. entered the first World War in 1917, 360,000 blacks, envigorated by their faith in democracy, put aside bitter memories of segregation and race violence and joined the fight for democracy. In New York City, the 15th Regiment of the New York National Guard made up of black soldiers (most of them from Harlem) was mustered into the regular Army, sent overseas to France and assigned to the French Army. Their regiment, renamed the 369th Infantry, was nicknamed the "Harlem Hellfighters." More than a hundred and fifty of these soldiers were decorated with the French Croix de Guerre, a military decoration for bravery.

After the War black soldiers returned to the United States with pride and a new sense of themselves and of their place in the world. They had fought side by side with black soldiers from other parts of the world. They had won the respect of foreign nations for their bravery. They returned with the hope that the spirit of democracy that they had fought for in Europe would await them in the United States.

"The Harlem Hellfighters"

Negro Soldiers
by Roscoe C. Jamison
The Crisis, September 1917

These truly are the Brave,
  These men who cast aside
Old memories, to walk the blood-stained
  pave
Of Sacrifice, joining the solemn tide
That moves away, to suffer and to die
For Freedom—when their own is yet denied!
O Pride! O Prejudice! When they pass by,
Hail them, the Brave, for you now crucified!

These truly are the Free,
These souls that grandly rise
Above base dreams of vengeance for their
  wrongs,
Who march to war with visions in their
  eyes
Of Peace through Brotherhood, lifting glad
  songs
Aforetime, while they front the firing-line.
Stand and behold! They take the field
  today,
Shedding their blood like Him now held
  divine,
That those who mock might find a better
  way!

The Call to Take Up the Pen

From their main offices in New York the National Association for the Advancement of Colored People (the NAACP) and the National Urban League disseminated the message of African American pride through their monthly magazines. W. E. B. Du Bois, editor of the NAACP's *The Crisis*, encouraged his readers to learn about their proud African heritage. Charles S. Johnson, editor of the Urban League's *Opportunity*, filled his magazine with news of successful African Americans from across the nation. These magazines offered literary contests and encouraged new writers to submit their works. The careers of many of the writers we associate with the Harlem Renaissance were launched by these magazines.

The Harlem of the twenties became a nurturing environment for young black writers. Writers like Langston Hughes, Zora Neale Hurston, Countee Cullen, Jean Toomer, and Jessie Fauset felt free to express their experiences and perspectives and to celebrate their African American heritage. The following poems are a small sample of some of their work created during this period.

W.E.B. Du Bois

Oriflamme
by Jessie Fauset
The Crisis, January 1920

"I can remember when I was a little, young girl, how my old mammy would sit out of doors in the evenings and look up at the stars and groan, and I would say, 'Mammy, what makes you groan so?" And she would say, 'I am groaning to think of my poor children; they do not know where I be and I don't know where they be. I look up at the stars and they look up at the stars!' "

—Sojourner Truth

I think I see her sitting bowed and black,
   Stricken and seared with slavery's
      mortal scars,
Reft of her children, lonely, anguished, yet
   Still looking at the stars.

Symbolic mother, we thy myriad sons,
   Pounding our stubborn hearts on Free-
      dom's bars,
Clutching our birthright, fight with faces
   set,
Still visioning the stars!

Saturday's Child
by Countee Cullen

Some are teethed on a silver spoon,
  With the stars strung for a rattle;
I cut my teeth as the black raccoon—
  For implements of battle.

Some are swaddled in silk and down,
  And heralded by a star;
They swathed my limbs in a sackcloth gown
  On a night that was black as tar.

For some, godfather and goddame
  The opulent fairies be;
Dame Poverty gave me my name,
  And Pain godfathered me.

For I was born on Saturday—
  "Bad time for planting a seed,"
Was all my father had to say,
  And, "One mouth more to feed."

Death cut the strings that gave me life,
  And handed me to Sorrow,
The only kind of middle wife
  My folks could beg or borrow.

The Negro Speaks of Rivers
by Langston Hughes

I've known rivers:
I've known rivers ancient as the world and older than the flow
   of human blood in human veins.

My soul has grown deep like the rivers.

I bathed in the Euphrates when dawns were young.
I built my hut near the Congo and it lulled me to sleep.
I looked upon the Nile and raised the pyramids above it.
I heard the singing of the Mississippi when Abe Lincoln went
   down to New Orleans, and I've seen its muddy bosom turn
   all golden in the sunset.

I've known rivers:
Ancient, dusky rivers.

My soul has grown deep like the rivers.

Song of the Son
by Jean Toomer

Pour O pour that parting soul in song,
O pour it in the sawdust glow of night,
Into the velvet pine-smoke air to-night,
And let the valley carry it along.
And let the valley carry it along.

O land and soil, red soil and sweet-gum tree,
So scant of grass, so profligate of pines,
Now just before an epoch's sun declines
Thy son, in time, I have returned to thee,
Thy son, I have in time returned to thee.

In time, for though the sun is setting on
A song-lit race of slaves, it has not set;
Though late, O soil, it is not too late yet
To catch thy plaintive soul, leaving, soon gone,
Leaving, to catch thy plaintive soul soon gone.

O Negro slaves, dark purple ripened plums,
Squeezed, and bursting in the pine-wood air,
Passing, before they stripped the old tree bare
One plum was saved for me, one seed becomes

An everlasting song, a singing tree,
Caroling softly souls of slavery,
What they were, and what they are to me,
Caroling softly souls of slavery.

The Lynching
by Claude McKay

His spirit in smoke ascended to high heaven.
His father, by the cruelest way of pain,
Had bidden him to his bosom once again;
The awful sin remained still unforgiven.
All night a bright and solitary star
(Perchance the one that ever guided him,
Yet gave him up at last to Fate's wild whim)
Hung pitifully o'er the swinging char.
Day dawned, and soon the mixed crowds came to view
The ghastly body swaying in the sun:
The women thronged to look, but never a one
Showed sorrow in her eyes of steely blue;
And little lads, lynchers that were to be,
Danced around the dreadful thing in fiendish glee.

The Debut of the Younger School of Negro Writers
Opportunity, May 1924

"Interest among the literati of New York in the emerging group of younger Negro writers found an expression in a recent meeting of the Writers' Guild, an informal group whose membership includes Countee Cullen, Eric Walrond, Langston Hughes, Jessie Fauset, Gwendolyn Bennett, Harold Jackman, Regina Anderson, and a few others. The occasion was a 'coming out party,' at the Civic Club, on March 21—a date selected around the appearance of the novel 'There Is Confusion' by Jessie Fauset. The responses to the invitations sent out were immediate and enthusiastic and the few regrets that came in were genuine.

"Although there was no formal, prearranged program, the occasion provoked a surprising spontaneity of expression both from the members of the writers' group and from the distinguished visitors present. . . .

"Dr. W E. B. Du Bois made his first public appearance and address since his return to this country from Africa. He was introduced by the chairman with soft seriousness as a representative of the "older school." Dr. Du Bois explained that the Negro writers of a few years back were of necessity pioneers, and much of their style was forced upon them by the barriers against publication of literature about Negroes of any sort.

"James Weldon Johnson was introduced as an anthologist of Negro verse and one who had given invaluable encouragement to the work of this younger group. . . .

"Another young Negro writer, Walter F. White, whose novel "Fire in Flint" has been accepted for publication, also spoke and made reference to the passing of the stereotypes of the Negroes of fiction.

"Professor Montgomery Gregory of Howard University, who came from Washington for the meeting, talked about the possibilities of Negroes in drama and told of the work of several talented Negro writers in this field, some of whose plays were just coming into recognition.

"Another visitor from Philadelphia, Dr. Albert C. Barnes, art connoisseur and foremost authority in America on primitive Negro art, sketched the growing interest in this art which had had such tremendous influence on the entire modern art movement.

"Miss Jessie Fauset was given a place of distinction on the program. She paid her respects to those friends who had contributed to her accomplishments, acknowledging a particular debt to her "best friend and severest critic," Dr. Du Bois.

"The original poems read by Countee Cullen were received with a tremendous ovation. Miss Gwendolyn Bennett's poem, dedicated to the occasion, is reproduced. It is called

'To Usward'

Let us be still
As ginger jars are still
Upon a Chinese shelf,
And let us be contained
By entities of Self. . . .

Not still with lethargy and sloth,
But quiet with the pushing of our growth;
Not self-contained with smug identity,
But conscious of the strength in entity.

If any have a song to sing that's different from
the rest,
Oh, let him sing before the urgency of Youth's
behest!

And some of us have songs to sing
Of jungle heat and fires;
And some of us are solemn grown
With pitiful desires;
And there are those who feel the pull
of seas beneath the skies;
And some there be who want to croon
Of Negro lullabies.
We claim no part with racial dearth,
We want to sing the songs of birth!

And so we stand like ginger jars,
Like ginger jars bound round
With dust and age;
Like jars of ginger we are sealed
By nature's heritage.
But let us break the seal of years
With pungent thrusts of song,
For there is joy in long dried tears,
For whetted passions of a throng!

A Voice for Separatism

A discussion of the Harlem Renaissance is not complete without mention of one other organization, and its colorful founder. In 1917, Marcus Garvey, a native of Jamaica and founder of the black nationalist movement, established the Universal Negro Improvement Association (UNIA). His was a message of black pride, but unlike that of Du Bois and other black leaders, Garvey preached separatism. Through his speeches and weekly newspaper, *The Negro World* (published in three languages), Garvey encouraged African Americans to establish their own economy separate from that of white capitalist America, and he offered blacks all over the world the vision of a new African homeland under black rule.

Garvey managed to get tremendous support from many blacks (in 1920, he boasted a membership of two million in thirty branches worldwide), but his flamboyant style and unorthodox business methods embarrassed and enraged many black intellectuals and black organizations. Garvey's movement began to lose momentum in 1925, when he was jailed for mail fraud and then deported to his home in Jamaica.

The Universal Negro Improvement Association: Speech at Liberty Hall, New York City (1922)

"Over five years ago the Universal Negro Improvement Association placed itself before the world as the movement through which the new and rising Negro would give expression of his feelings. This Association adopts an attitude not of hostility to other races and peoples of the world, but an attitude of self-respect.

". . .Wheresoever human rights are denied to any group, wheresoever justice is denied to any group, there the U.N.I.A. finds a cause. And at this time among all the peoples of the world, the group that suffers most from injustice, the group that is denied most of those rights that belong to all humanity, is the black group. . . even so under the leadership of the U.N.I.A., we are marshaling the 400,000,000 Negroes of the world to fight for the emancipation of the race and of the redemption of the country of our fathers.

"We represent a new line of thought among Negroes. Whether you call it advanced thought or reactionary thought, I do not care. If it is reactionary for people to seek independence in government, then we are reactionary. If it is advanced thought for people to seek liberty and freedom, then we represent the advanced school of thought among the Negroes of this country. We of the U.N.I.A. believe that what is good for the other folks is good for us. If Government is something that is worth while; if government is something that is appreciable and helpful and protective to others, then we also want to experiment in government. We do not mean a government that will make us citizens without rights or subjects without consideration. We mean a kind of government that will place our race in control, even as other races are in control of their own government.

"...The U.N.I.A. is not advocating the cause of church building, because we have a sufficiently large number of churches among us to minister to the spiritual needs of the people, and we are not going to compete with those who are engaged in so splendid a work; we are not engaged in building any new social institutions,... because there are enough social workers engaged in those praiseworthy efforts. We are not engaged in politics because we have enough local politicians, ...and the political situation is well taken care of. We are not engaged in domestic politics, in church building or in social uplift work, but we are engaged in nation building.

"In advocating the principles of this Association we find we have been very much misunderstood and very much misrepresented by men from within our own race, as well as others from without. Any reform movement that seeks to bring about changes for the benefit of humanity is bound to be misrepresented by those who have always taken it upon themselves to administer to, and lead the unfortunate...

"...The Universal Negro Improvement Association stands for the Bigger Brotherhood; the Universal Negro Improvement Association stands for human rights,

Marcus Garvey

not only for Negroes, but for all races. The Universal Negro Improvement Association believes in the rights of not only the black race, but the white race, the yellow race and the brown race. The Universal Negro Improvement Association believes that the white man has as much right to be considered, the yellow man has as much right to be considered, the brown man has as much right to be considered as the black man of Africa. In view of the fact that the black man of Africa has contributed as much to the world as the white man of Europe, and the brown man and yellow man of Asia, we of the Universal Negro Improvement Association demand that the white, yellow and brown races give to the black man his place in the civilization of the world. We ask for nothing more than the rights of 400,000,000 Negroes. We are not seeking, as I said before, to destroy or disrupt the society of the government of other races, but we are determined that 400,000,000 of us shall unite ourselves to free our motherland from the grasp of the invader. . .

"The Universal Negro Improvement Association is not seeking to build up another government within the bounds or borders of the United States of America. The Universal Negro Improvement Association is not seeking to disrupt any organized system of government, but the Association is determined to bring Negroes together for the building up of a nation of their own. And why? Because we have been forced to it. We have been forced to it throughout the world; not only in America, not only in Europe, not only in the British

Empire, but wheresoever the black man happens to find himself, he has been forced to do for himself.

"To talk about Government is a little more than some of our people can appreciate... The average man... seems to say, 'Why should there be need for any other government?' We are French, English or American. But we of the U.N.I.A. have studied seriously this question of nationality among Negroes—this American nationality, this British nationality, this French, Italian or Spanish nationality, and have discovered that it counts for nought when that nationality comes in conflict with the racial idealism of the group that rules. When our interests clash with those of the ruling faction, then we find that we have absolutely no rights. In times of peace, when everything is all right, Negroes have a hard time, wherever we go, wheresoever we find ourselves, getting those rights that belong to us in common with others whom we claim as fellow citizens; getting that consideration that should be ours by right of the constitution, by right of the law; but in the time of trouble they make us all partners in the cause, as happened in the last war...

"We have saved many nations in this manner, and we have lost our lives doing that before. Hundreds of thousands—nay, millions of black men, lie buried under the ground due to that old-time camouflage of saving the nation. We saved the British Empire; we saved the French Empire; we saved this glorious country more than once; and all that we have received for our sacrifices, all that we have received for what we have done, even in giving up our lives, is just what you are receiving now, just what I am receiving now.

"You and I fare no better in America, in the British Empire, or any other part of the white world; we fare no better than any black man wheresoever he shows his head...

"The U.N.I.A. is reversing the old-time order of things. We refuse to be followers anymore. We are leading ourselves. That means, if any saving is to be done,... .we are going to seek a method of saving Africa first. Why? And why Africa? Because Africa has become the grand prize of the nations. Africa has become the big game of the nation hunters. Today Africa looms as the greatest commercial, industrial and political prize in the world.

"The difference between the Universal Negro Improvement Association and the other movements of this country, and probably the world, is that the Universal Negro Improvement Association seeks independence of government, while the other organizations seek to make the Negro a secondary part of existing governments. We differ from the organizations in America because they seek to subordinate the Negro as a secondary consideration in a great civilization, knowing that in America the Negro will never reach his highest ambition, knowing that the Negro in America will never get his constitutional rights. All other organizations which are fostering the improvement of Negroes in the British Empire know that the Negro in the British Empire will never reach the height of his constitutional rights. What do I mean by constitutional rights in America? If the black man is to reach the height of his ambition in this country—if the black man is to get all of his constitutional rights in America—then the black man should have the same chance in the nation as any other man to become president of the nation, or a street cleaner in New York. If the black man in the British Empire is to have all his constitutional rights it means that the Negro in the British Empire should have at least the same right to become premier of Great Britain as he has to become street cleaner in the city of London. Are they prepared to give us such political equality? You and I can live in the United States of America for 100 more years, and our generations may live for 200 years or for 5000 more years, and so long as there is a black and white population, when the majority is on the side of the white race, you and I will never get political justice or get political equality in this country. Then why should a black man with rising ambition, after preparing himself in every possible way to give expression to that highest ambition, allow himself to be kept down by racial prejudice within a country? If I am as educated as the next man, if I am as prepared as the next man, if I have passed through the best schools and colleges and universities as the other fellow, why should I not have a fair chance to compete with the other fellow for the biggest position in the nation?. . .

"We are not preaching a propaganda of hate against anybody. We love the white man; we love all humanity. . . The white man is as necessary to the existence of the Negro as the Negro is necessary to his existence. There is a common relationship that we cannot escape. Africa has certain things that Europe wants, and Europe has certain things that Africa wants, . . . it is impossible for us to escape it. Africa has oil, diamonds, copper, gold and rubber and all the minerals that Europe wants, and there must be some kind of relationship between Africa and Europe for a fair exchange, so we cannot afford to hate anybody.

"The question often asked is what does it require to redeem a race and free a country? If it takes man power, if it takes scientific intelligence, if it takes education of any kind, or if it takes blood, then the 400,000,000 Negroes of the world have it.

"It took the combined power of the Allies to put down the mad determination of the Kaiser to impose German will upon the world and upon humanity. Among those who suppressed his mad ambition were two million Negroes who have not yet forgotten how to drive men across the firing line. . . when so many white men refused to answer to the call and dodged behind all kinds of excuses, 400,000 black men were ready without a question. It was because we were told it was a war of democracy; it was a war for the liberation of the weaker peoples of the world. We heard the cry of Woodrow Wilson, not because we liked him so, but because the things he said were of such a nature that they appealed to us as men. Wheresoever the cause of humanity stands in need of assistance, there you will find the Negro ever ready to serve.

"He has done it from the time of Christ up to now. When the whole world turned its back upon the

Christ, the man who was said to be the Son of God, when the world cried out 'Crucify Him,' when the world spurned Him and spat upon Him, it was a black man, Simon, the Cyrenian, who took up the cross. Why? Because the cause of humanity appealed to him. When the black man saw the suffering Jew, struggling under the heavy cross, he was willing to go to His assistance, and he bore that cross up to the heights of Calvary. In the spirit of Simon, the Cyrenian, 1900 years ago, we answered the call of Woodrow Wilson, the call to a larger humanity, and it was for that that we willingly rushed into the war. . .

"We shall march out, yes, as black American citizens, as black British subjects, as black French citizens, as black Italians or as black Spaniards, but we shall march out with a greater loyalty, the loyalty of race. We shall march out in answer to the cry of our fathers, who cry out to us for the redemption of our own country, our motherland, Africa.

"We shall march out, not forgetting the blessings of America. We shall march out, not forgetting the blessings of civilization. We shall march out with a history of peace before and behind us, and surely that history shall be our breast-plate, for how can man fight better than knowing that the cause for which he fights is righteous?. . . Glorious shall be the battle when the time comes to fight for our people and our race.

"We should say to the millions who are in Africa to hold the fort, for we are coming 400,000,000 strong."

New Rhythms

The rhythms of the blues and the syncopated beats of jazz which had been carried northward from the black south developed into the musical sounds of Harlem. These new sounds played out at theatres and at the many nightclubs that sprouted up in Harlem. One of the most famous clubs was the Cotton Club where "whites only" audiences were treated to the talents of black performers such as Cab Calloway and Duke Ellington. Black audiences, meanwhile, would catch their favorite acts at smaller clubs like Edmund's Cellar or Leroy's or at the popular "rent parties" where the music would continue till dawn.

The Weary Blues
by Langston Hughes

Droning a drowsy syncopated tune,
Rocking back and forth to a mellow croon,
    I heard a Negro play.
Down on Lenox Avenue the other night
By the pale dull pallor of an old gas light
    He did a lazy sway. . . .
    He did a lazy sway. . . .
To the tune o' those Weary Blues.
With his ebony hands on each ivory key
He made that poor piano moan with melody.
    O Blues!
Swaying to and fro on his rickety stool
He played that sad raggy tune like a musical fool.
    Sweet Blues!
Coming from a black man's soul.
    O Blues!
In a deep song voice with a melancholy tone
I heard that Negro sing, that old piano moan—
    "Ain't got nobody in all this world,
    Ain't got nobody but ma self.
    I's gwine to quit ma frownin'
    And put ma troubles on the shelf."
Thump, thump, thump, went his foot on the floor.
He played a few chords then he sang some more—
    "I got the Weary Blues
    And I can't be satisfied.
    Got the Weary Blues
    And can't be satisfied—
    I ain't happy no mo'
    And I wish that I had died."
And far into the night he crooned that tune.
The stars went out and so did the moon.
The singer stopped playing and went to bed
While the Weary Blues echoed through his head.
He slept like a rock or a man that's dead.

Dream Deferred

The spirit of the Harlem of the twenties provided a colorful backdrop for this creative explosion of Black art we know as the Harlem Renaissance. Yet in the thirties, that backdrop fell heavily with the Great Depression.

The promise that glowed during the Harlem Renaissance was obscured by a harsher light of reality. Publishing and performing opportunities decreased as money became scarce everywhere. Writers became more preoccupied with the social and economic realities and their themes displayed little of the hope and optimisim of earlier works.

Harlem
by Langston Hughes

What happens to a dream deferred?

> Does it dry up
> like a raisin in the sun?
> Or fester like a sore—
> And then run?
> Does it stink like rotten meat?
> Or crust and sugar over
> like a syrupy sweet?
>
> Maybe it just sags
> like a heavy load.
>
> *Or does it explode?*

Definitions

boll weevil – a small grayish beetle with destructive larvae that damages the seed pod of the cotton plant.

Crispus Attucks (1723-1770) – believed to be a runaway slave. Was the first man to die in the American Revolution at the Boston Massacre, March 5, 1770.

Frederick Douglas (1817-1895) – escaped slavery in 1838. He was a well-known lecturer for the anti-slavery movement, a writer and a publisher. He held the position of U.S. Minister to Haiti in 1889.

Jim Crow – refers to practices, laws and institutions that support segregation of Blacks from Whites. The term came into use in the late nineteenth century when racial segregation was made legal in the South. Jim Crow was the name of a black character in a popular song composed in 1830.

Ku Klux Klan – a secret society organized in Tennessee in 1866 that used violence to reassert white supremacy.

lynching – to kill a person by mob action, usually by hanging, without due process of law.

rent parties – parties given at private apartments, but guests were required to pay admission fees supposedly to help the tenant pay the rent. The guests were usually treated to live music and refreshments.

sharecropper – a tenant farmer who gives a share of his crop to a landowner as payment for renting the land.

Sojourner Truth (1797-1883) – a former slave whose original name was Isabella Baumfree. She was a preacher, abolitionist and lecturer who spoke against slavery and injustice.

Wendell Phillips (1811-1884) – abolitionist, lawyer and social reformer. A graduate of Harvard, he was a chief orator of the Antislavery Society.

Bibliography

Adoff, Arnold, ed. *I Am the Darker Brother – An Anthology of Modern Poems by Black Americans*, The Macmillan Company, New York, 1968.

Anderson, Jervis, *This Was Harlem – A Cultural Portrait 1900-1950*, Farrar Strauss Giroux, New York, 1982.

Early, Gerald, ed. *My Soul's High Song: The Collected Writings of Countee Cullen, Voice of the Harlem Renaissance*, Doubleday, New York, 1991.

"Harlem Renaissance Bibliography for Adults," *Booklist*, ALA Publishing Committee, Chicago, February 1, 1992.

Honey, Maureen, ed. *Shadowed Dreams – Women's Poetry of the Harlem Renaissance*, Rutgers University Press, New Brunswick and London, 1989.

Huggins, Nathan Irvin, *Voices From The Harlem Renaissance*, Oxford University Press, New York, 1976.

Hughes, Langston and Arna Bontemps, ed. *The Poetry of the Negro 1746-1970*, Doubleday & Company, New York, 1970.

Johnson, James Weldon, ed. *The Book of American Negro Poetry*, Harcourt Brace & World, Inc., 1922.

Levering, David Lewis, *When Harlem Was in Vogue*, Oxford, 1981.

Ploski, Harry A. and James Williams, ed. *The Negro Almanac: A Reference Work on the African American*, Gale Research, Inc., Detroit, 1989.

Southern, Eileen, *The Music of Black Americans – A History*, W.W. Norton and Co., New York, 1971.

Toomer, Jean, *Cane*, Liveright Publishing Corp., New York, 1975.

Wintz, Cary D., *Black Culture and the Harlem Renaissance*, Rice University, 1988.

About the Author

Kathryn Cryan-Hicks lives in Chelmsford, Massachusetts with her husband and three young children. She currently works at the Chelmsford Public Library as the Head of Community Services, but for over six years worked in the library's Reference Department. She has also worked in the fields of Employee Communications and Public Relations. Her first book, a biography, *W. E. B. Du Bois: Crusader for Peace* was also published by Discovery Enterprises, Ltd.